First World War
and Army of Occupation
War Diary
France, Belgium and Germany

60 DIVISION
Divisional Troops
Royal Army Medical Corps
2/4 London Field Ambulance
15 June 1916 - 30 November 1916

WO95/3029/3

The Naval & Military Press Ltd
www.nmarchive.com
Published in association with The National Archives

Published by

The Naval & Military Press Ltd

Unit 10 Ridgewood Industrial Park,

Uckfield, East Sussex,

TN22 5QE England

Tel: +44 (0) 1825 749494

www.naval-military-press.com

www.nmarchive.com

This diary has been reprinted in facsimile from the original. Any imperfections are inevitably reproduced and the quality may fall short of modern type and cartographic standards.

© Crown Copyright
Images reproduced by permission of The National Archives, London, England, 2015.

Contents

Document type	Place/Title	Date From	Date To
Heading	WO95/3029/2		
Heading	War Diary of 2/4 London Field Ambulance from 15th 1916 to July 31st		
War Diary	Sutton Veny	15/06/1916	22/06/1916
War Diary	Warminster	22/06/1916	22/06/1916
War Diary	Southampton	22/06/1916	22/06/1916
War Diary	Havre	23/06/1916	24/06/1916
War Diary	Abbeville	24/06/1916	25/06/1916
War Diary	St Pol	25/06/1916	25/06/1916
War Diary	Maizieres	26/06/1916	02/07/1916
War Diary	ACQ	02/07/1916	13/07/1916
War Diary	Ecoivres	13/07/1916	19/07/1916
War Diary	Light	19/07/1916	25/07/1916
War Diary	Ecoivres	25/07/1916	30/07/1916
War Diary	Aurietz	30/07/1916	30/07/1916
War Diary	Ecoivres	30/07/1916	31/07/1916
Heading	War Diary Vol 3 Pages 10 to 14 of Major B. Layton, Commanding 2/4th London Field Ambulance.		
Heading	War Diary. Vol III. Appendiix I 2/4 London Field Ambce. Organization On Advanced Dressing Sation.		
Miscellaneous			
Miscellaneous	Para 2		
Diagram etc	Advanced Dressing Station.		
Miscellaneous	Para 3		
War Diary	Econres	01/08/1916	31/08/1916
Heading	War Diary Of 2/4 London Field Ambulance Vol III Pgs 15-19 September 1916		
War Diary	Ecoivres	01/09/1916	30/09/1916
Heading	60th Div 2/4th London Field Ambulance Oct 1916		
Heading	War Diary of 2/4th London Field Ambulance from Oct 1916 to Oct 31st 1916 Vol III		
War Diary	Ecoivres	01/10/1916	05/10/1916
Miscellaneous	Memo On Advanced Dressing Station And Collecting Posts. App 2	02/10/1916	02/10/1916
War Diary	Ecoivres	06/10/1916	24/10/1916
War Diary	ACQ	24/10/1916	24/10/1916
War Diary	Berles	24/10/1916	24/10/1916
War Diary	Mont-En-Ternois	24/10/1916	28/10/1916
War Diary	Fortel	28/10/1916	29/10/1916
War Diary	Prouville	29/10/1916	31/10/1916
Miscellaneous	Medical Arrangements for 179th Brigade and attached troops for the period 8 a.m. 28th October 1916 till morning of October 29th. app III	27/10/1916	27/10/1916
Heading	2/4th London F.A.		
Heading	War Diary of 2/4 London Field Ambulance From Nov 1st 1916 To Nov 30th 1916 Volume III		
War Diary	Prouville	01/11/1916	03/11/1916
War Diary	St Riquier	03/11/1916	03/11/1916
War Diary	Eaucourt Sur Somme	03/11/1916	14/11/1916
War Diary	Longpre	14/11/1916	14/11/1916

War Diary	Montereau	15/11/1916	15/11/1916
War Diary	Macon	16/11/1916	16/11/1916
War Diary	Vienne	16/11/1916	16/11/1916
War Diary	Pierrette	16/11/1916	16/11/1916
War Diary	Marseilles	17/11/1916	19/11/1916
War Diary	At Sea	20/11/1916	29/11/1916
War Diary	Salonika	30/11/1916	30/11/1916
Miscellaneous	179th Brigade And Attached Troops. App 304	02/11/1916	02/11/1916
War Diary	Daily Diary of M.O. i/c troops A.M.T. "Transylvania' appendix 5	19/11/1916	30/11/1916
Miscellaneous	H.M.I Transylvania	30/11/1916	30/11/1916
Miscellaneous	H.M.T Transylvania		
Miscellaneous	H.M.T Transylvania	30/11/1916	30/11/1916
Miscellaneous	Notes on Evacuation of Wounded in the Neuville St. Vaast Area by the 2/4th London Field Ambulance June to October 1916		

WO 95/3029/2

MEDICAL 60

Army Form C. 2118.

Vol I II

WAR DIARY
or
INTELLIGENCE SUMMARY.
(Erase heading not required.)

CONFIDENTIAL

War Diary
of
2/1st London Fld Ambulance

from June 15th 1916
(date of first mobilization)
to July 31st

(Volume I)

COMMITTEE FOR THE
MEDICAL HISTORY OF THE WAR
Date 13 SEP. 1916

MEDICAL.

Vol III page 1.   2/4 LOND. AMB.   Army Form C. 2118.

WAR DIARY
or
INTELLIGENCE SUMMARY.
(Erase heading not required.)

Hour, Date, Place	Summary of Events and Information	Remarks and references to Appendices
SUTTON VENY		
15.VI.16. THURS.	Receipt of mobilization orders. T.B.L.	SECTION
16.VI.16. FRI.	Complete inspection of all men with clothing, accoutrements, equipment, all horses, harness and G.S. waggons. T.B.L.	Special work for officers.
17.VI.16. SAT.	Return of stores not being taken overseas. T.B.L.	Capt/s B. E.P. ANNETT Sanitary & water expert
18.VI.16. SUN.	Went to Holyday. Church parade - packing up of all private property. T.B.L.	A. G.R. SPENCER M.O. to unit - expert in infectious diseases
19.VI.16. MON.	C.O's in morning tot Thursday. - Route march - Body clothes inspection afternoon. - Lecture to joined officers on gas attack. - Lecture to all officers N.C.O's on branches & contagion diseases of army. T.B.L.	C. L. PRICE HARRIS acting A.S.T.
20.VI.16 TUES.	Col in morning - cert day. - Scrutinizing of kits & other fatigues - in afternoon sanitary parade - inspection of gas helmets - 1st aid dressings. - Identity discs - Disciplinary & other parades. Gives standing orders & readouts to all on parade. T.B.L.	C. G.B. PRITCHARD 6% morning
		C. E. PETLEY R.M.Sec. officers
21.VI.16. WED.	Fire and morning - preliminary med order issued (unsigned) J.M.A. 7MB.	B. L. MILTON assistant to % morning
		BRD 1st Brigade gas expert
		B. W.J.T. KIMBER % all Bathing, Laundry A. & personal cleanliness arrangements for 2/4 LOND. AMB.

2/4 LOND. AMB.

Army Form C. 2118.

WAR DIARY
or
INTELLIGENCE SUMMARY.
(Erase heading not required.)

Vol III ps 2.

Instructions regarding War Diaries and Intelligence Summaries are contained in F.S. Regs., Part II and the Staff Manual respectively. Title pages will be prepared in manuscript.

Hour, Date, Place	Summary of Events and Information	Remarks and references to Appendices
SUTTON VENY 21.vi.16 11.30am 5.0pm	Fine but cool. Tried inspection of all units fully equipped. J.P.L. Medical inspection of all units. Lending efforts, handing over stores detailed. J.P.L.	
22.vi.16 1.45am 2.45am 5.32am 6.23am 6.22am	Reveille. Breakfast – 3.45am. Parade – 4.15am. Moved off. J.P.L. Roll called in presence of Capt. P. LE BRETON – all present. J.P.L. Fine day becoming hot. Water. J.P.L. Arrived at station. Train ready for loading 6.10am. Loaded wagons & horses on. J.P.L. Personnel on train. Began to make up train 6.30am. Train off 7.19L.	
WARMINSTER SOUTHAMPTON 9.10am arrived 11.15	All wagons & horses on board. – Capt. & Lieut. WETT with S.S. INVENTOR – 3 officers 68 other ranks all details three on S.S. CONNAUGHT – 5.45pm S.S. CONNAUGHT. All armament personnel on S.S. CONNAUGHT. Fine rain. J.P.L. Moved off. Smooth passage. No rain. J.P.L.	
23.vi.16 HAVRE	0.15am arrived 7.50am all off S.S. CONNAUGHT – began raining again – and continued off and on till 11.0pm. – men getting aboard in queue. 9.30 till 8.0 into a hopper at 12 noon. – Disembarking officers (not many) R.E. cycles on top of this place. Men who were waiting coffee horses – some invaliding civilians – lost lock on and 11.40 moved off. 13.40 – arrived at Rest Camp 15.40 fine evening at first Showers. J.P.L.	
24.vi.16 6.0am	Reveille. Issued hot stews breakfast 8.0am – Parade 9.0am. 2nd parade 11.35am moved off 11.50am arrived entraining point 13.30pm. Train left 16.11pm. – Hot day – two who Hill is spirited services J.P.L. All gas helmets to hand tested with day of issue. J.P.L.	

(73989) W4141–463. 400,000. 9/14. H.&J.Ltd. Forms/C. 2118/10.

2/L LOND. AMB. Vol III / PS. 3.

Army Form C. 2118.

WAR DIARY
or
~~INTELLIGENCE~~ SUMMARY
(Erase heading not required.)

Ref. map II. intro LENS.

Instructions regarding War Diaries and Intelligence Summaries are contained in F.S. Regs., Part II and the Staff Manual respectively. Title pages will be prepared in manuscript.

Hour, Date, Place	Summary of Events and Information	Remarks and references to Appendices
ABBEVILLE 8.15 a.m. 25.VI.16	arrived – horses watered – tea & rations issued 7.15 /	
ST POL 12.15 p.m.	arrived – detained by 12.30 – half day – 7.V.54.	
MAIZIÈRES 6.15 p.m.	arrived – unit luggage & motor tyres – dinner issued 8 p.m. – ecroasvaillie from 179 N°B°A & attached troops J.R.A.	
26.VI.16 10 a.m.	repeated Shurtan beginning work Sunday. Capt PETLEY took cncl of 2/h Coy RE & 5/180y ACS. (Inf) – 2 admittees from Nc North – O.C. reported troubles at 5 pm – temp 2 Coys' 2 Bn G of 11.30 am. J.R.A.	
27.VI.16	receiving in afternoon – word from bath – tea to Sister form at Bruno P°A. N.B. great difficulty in watering horse line 3½ mts to T Pn. T.L.
4.30 p.m.	ac visited B°A Stationary Hospital at 1.70 PM – Hq Staff arrived 6°B° 62 CCS AUBIGNY T°A.	
	L. Sgt BIRD – Cpl DENVON 8 pte. detailed 67° 62 CCS AUBIGNY T°A.	
28.VI.16	still raining – Capt PRICE HARRIS reported to ½ Highland Field Amb ECOIVRES wen ACS	
2.10 p.m.	C section	
	for instrn – 4 p.m. A.D.M.S. Jr Dvns visited in. Jnt.	
29.VI.16	free day – v.c. writes D.H.O. VILLARS CHATEL – DDMS 17° Corps Came Down in afternoon. T.L.	
30.VI.16	Rain warning – motorcycle damaged in afternoon	

WAR DIARY
INTELLIGENCE SUMMARY

2/4 LOND. AMB. vsIII PS 4. Army Form C. 2118.

Ref. LENS 1/40000

Hour, Date, Place	Summary of Events and Information	Remarks and references to Appendices
MAIZIERES 1.VII.16 2.VII.16 10 am	Fine hot day – Kit fast, boots & hot water for bath "woke" fitted up with hospitalin as a bath for heatspot Details 7nsh. Church parade for all – word of hospital – meeting of officers after catechism by Orders strength 7nsh.	
A.C.Q. 9.15 pm 3.VII.16	on arrival traineys him to get in ambulance – in huts during R.E. Church Parade by French 7nsh. First ambulance arrived – First half Day 7nsh.	
8.20 pm 3/6	Fine Day – all busy cleaning camp – it has been used by nine Infantry Brough, and as a result had got in bad state. Horse shelter washed out with Quick lime to present smells – no longer used by For Trucks 7nsh.	
8.5 pm	report little ready for for Trucks 7nsh. returned to oc/2 Highland Hand. where 'C' Section is to	A (5/3)(8c)
9.0 pm	remain 7nsh. went up to the ow. A.D.S. at AU RIETZ (1:40000 5/3)(8c) where Capts PRICE HARRIS & PRITCHARD were at work, all any were tent planned at least to 8 at work exclusive of any were already amongst them. 7.18 h.	
10.9 pm L. VII. 20 Cm 10.0 am	before leaving Heavy thunderstorm – 7nsh. Reported to Adms 56 Div – rest ADMS body also returned to our camp. Work continued from afternoon around NK. Ebouridring for 10 founds in the huts. Thos. ow lectures the at attempt today now deep lecture hut traits learning on	

2/4 LOND. AMB.

WAR DIARY
or
INTELLIGENCE SUMMARY.
(Erase heading not required.)

Army Form C. 2118.

vol III P.S. 5.

Ref LENS 1/100000 unless otherwise mentioned

Hour, Date, Place	Summary of Events and Information	Remarks and references to Appendices
ACO. 5.VII.16 5 p.m.	Capt. E. MINETT - MILTON & KIMBER with B section and ford from A section detached for instruction to 1/3 Highland branch HAUTE AVESNES to instructor at D.R.S. Capts. PRICE HARRIS - PRITCHARD - PETHEY with 'C' section returned from instruction with 1/3 Highland Fourd 2 m.t. wth Pte. LUCAS visited MAROEUIL thence by I.V.Y rived to Cue RIETZ - + back by car at 10 p.m. rain continued 7 m.z.	
6.VII.16 7.VII.16	work in camp continued - rain continued 7 m.z. work in camp cont'd - snow falling throughout 7 m.z. visited 1/3 Highland 7 Am.b. HAUTE AVESNES - Divl S/Waters XVII Corps camp round D.S. J.P.t.	
8.VII.16	wth Sergt. Major & Pte. LUCAS visited around Trenches AURIETZ - A.D.S. - 513.) A.9. d.2.5 - MAISON BLANCHE - Brigade H.Q. (Major 1/10000) Post CENTRAY & TARGETTE - NEVILLE St VAAST - Aux posts of Caura sector 1/4 Cavl adv S. - wrk in camp cont'd - wet day 7 m.z.	
9.VII.16	Church parade — Capt KIMBER — 33 men returned — Capt SPENCER 4/6 O.R. reports to Capt MINETT who then reported to O.C. 1/1 Highland Field Aml. 1/cs for instruction with his party — fine day — with A.D.M.S returned. 7 m.z.	
10.VII.16	A.D.M.S came round. Fine day — went to BRAY hotel with R. STAFF. 1179 & advising them on sanitation. Town Major + to BRAY hotel with R. STAFF in evening - consulted H & E (visits) 3/4 H & 7/4 L. Aml. in evening. 2 men Capt MINETT 7. m.z.	
11.VII.16	Sanct. Sanitary monthly to half Town Major - Sergt. K. Parkes, wounded + half Staff 179 9/R.S. - Fine day - 1/3 Trenches - NEVILLE St VAAST - R.A.P.S. Cap. Tractor returned by AURIETZ - arrangements for fortnight 7 m.z.	

2/1 LOND. AMB. WAR DIARY 1st VIII Pg 6. Army Form C. 2118.

INTELLIGENCE SUMMARY
(Erase heading not required.) Ref LENS 1/100,000 enclosed Brussels new series

Hour, Date, Place	Summary of Events and Information	Remarks and references to Appendices
A.C.O. 12.VII.16 8.45 A.M.	Capt PETTEY &1 O.R. went off to NEUVILLE a.D.S. AURIETZ – POT CENTRALE posted NEUVILLE ST VAAST – & replace personnel of 2/3 HIGHLAND F.AMB. of R.A.P. & left & couts sector – Fine day 7PL.	
12.noon	7 O.R. returned from Capt MINETT 7PL.	
2.0 pm	S/Sgt ROMAINE 190.R. wounded (staff A.D.S. 7PL.)	
6.0 pm	Capt SPENCER 4 O.R. returned from Capt MINETT. 7PL.	
8.10 pm	Capt KIMBER 2 O.R. & MAROEUIL & on R.A.P. Herg 20 R. (wounded) 7PL.	
8.35 pm	wounded & 1 S. wagon & amb. to take up equipment to A.D.S. & other posts. 2.13'L	
11.0 pm	arrived A.U. RIETZ 7PL.	
11.30 pm	relief completed 7PL.	
9.0 pm	Capt PRICE HARRIS took on wagon undressers at BRAY – 3 cars same(NT)	
	4 O.R. Rang – returned there 7PL.	Fine day 7PL
13.VII.16 2.15 am	Reported relief completed BAJOMS (A.D.S. R.A.P.S) 7PL.	
	everyone in the duties – Fine day 7PL.	
8.0 am	Capt MILTON 30 O.R. returned from Capt MINETT 7PL.	
10.0 am	Capt BIRD reports his return to 30/2 C.C.S. from 3/III C.C.S. 7PL.	
12 noon	Capt MINETT reports return 7PL.	
2.30 pm	Left A.C.O. 7PL.	
	onward &going 7PL. – Found D.S. full of sick & wounded undergoing attended to in & – Capt& PRICE HARRIS & MILTON worked very hard setting	
ECOIVRES 3.0 pm	up M.D.S. and attending there working well. 7PL.	
	abt 6pm – evacuation from there working well. 7PL.	
16.VII.16 8.30 am	had only 10 cases available for general work on Rams in vicinity of M.D.S. – Capt MINETT depended on duty at examinations with Sani Pak – & ECOIVRES – 2 mins to half hour with extra help when needed of MAROEUIL – Fine day. – & MAROEUIL in afternoon – attended 7PL. uncertain –	

Army Form C. 2118.

WAR DIARY
or
INTELLIGENCE SUMMARY.
(Erase heading not required.) Pol LENS / (area unless otherwise stated)

2/1 LOND. AMB. VIII 157

Instructions regarding War Diaries and Intelligence Summaries are contained in F.S. Regs., Part II and the Staff Manual respectively. Title pages will be prepared in manuscript.

Hour, Date, Place	Summary of Events and Information	Remarks and references to Appendices
ECON RES. 15.VII	This Day - nothing to rept.	
16.VII	Hot + calm - church parade - 2 arms wound 0/R Sexton + Melville	
	St. VAAST. JPL	
17.VII	visit OOZMA JPL	
	Capt KIMBER relieved Capt SPENCER at ADS 2nh/	
18.VII	Tues day - Capt PRICE HARRIS - PRITCHARD - MILTON to 1st Pol to be relieved	
19	SMS 3rd Army — Capt PRITCHARD relieved Capt RETLEY at ADS. —	
	Got up to the woods 1/3 aunx between BRAY & MAROEUIL - car came	
	work duet from MDS - "Good" grub truck early for a week or so	
	- reported to Lt unfind com shall try wine from 200 & org 180 F3 at	
	AIRIEZ JPL.	
night 19–20.VII	Went round MDN section & DST centrale - proposed breakdowns h?	
	Ikemans wit with RAF to h Jpl.	
20.VII	Tues day - change of personnel OR. and up the line - very hard to manage	
	as till then some back there is a wound tracery or at MDS. - 1rd.	
	large trucks been is u wind brought into use - Tues day JPL	
21.VII	Actine. saw team - water derly flower - instruction in training JPL.	
22.VII	Sunday - Church parade w wound - free day - within truck JPL.	
23.VII	BOZMA visited MDS - [?] planned with them JPL.	
	This day - visited OC AMBALLA FAB Amb'ce - Capt PRICE HARRIS	
24.VII	and MILTON relieve Capt PRITCHARD NUMBER at ADS.	
	visited Fm G.O.C. - discussed the banks owing toward - address't huts	
25.VII	at the beach - to be allotted us - my cnterval of [?] trying to get	
	it furnishd - have not thrid wearing accommodation for patients	
	G Gerard Cucency — We are to plan for us with accurate JPL	

2/4 LOND. AMB.   WAR DIARY   Vol VIII/pg 9   Army Form C. 2118.
or
INTELLIGENCE SUMMARY.   Ref 26 IVS related nuclear/chemical studies
(Erase heading not required.)

Hour, Date, Place	Summary of Events and Information	Remarks and references to Appendices

ÉCOIVRES 25.VIII cont.

3 p.m. — Lt. C.R.E. re enemy — enough to off chances. TMC
5 p.m. — A/c cmdg in air allotted 3 huts — wanted to truck out/scam some night — informed. TMC

26.VII — Running MONT ST ELOY — HATBS(?)ETTE road — not better. Most of movement seen to caucen. Three 6 RMP oreto —
Explosn trouble between stockpiling line to P.I. if working
party could get own dog out fast to shelter the distance
Evacuation turn this point. TMC
evacuation inspn at cdps — round trucks to Meerts RAP.

10.30 am Saw Mjrs 14, 16 Batts, arranged with them about moving TMC
3 p.m. — DDMS & ADMS — round MDS — and of clearing news huts

27.VII — turn round continued began these TMC
28.VII — clearing huts, cmps — ADMS, others in b/sups to/from in town TMC
— Inspect depts — Cap PETLEY exports — ADMS for conference
outpns defence — evacuation Ly nfly nns with ... LA

TARGETTE — MONT ST ELOY — scene of cars turning infants
ADS. — Things in auxiliary arms — TMC. always appreciating individual wounded —
29.VII — visit by DMS, 3 Army. Discussed future of keeping long benn — Enemy — meeting in
it's use in case of new infanteries. [Guerchin evening — place offices coming through in hills of. 27-28.
continued TMC 28-29
29-30
TMC

30.VII — Revisited MEUVILLE ST VAAST from hmlt
9:30 am — to ADS. Issue — mis by evening — Thence RAP. P.sector —
view of huts just up — CdeS — on by evening — Thence — c.dep. O. Sector anyone
discussed fnsl with TR M.O. — Thence to front-line trench by
a/trps — soma to Wsector — Sp'm to front-line trench by
Lt Col ? ... New Capt ZADELL. M.O. thence back to A D S.

WAR DIARY *or* **INTELLIGENCE SUMMARY.**
(Erase heading not required.)

3/1 LOND AMB.   vol IV. pg 89

Army Form C. 2118.

R/ LENS /1/0.V.11

Hour, Date, Place	Summary of Events and Information	Remarks and references to Appendices
Hu RIETZ 30.V.11 10 a.m.	Learnt from the a.d.s. that ways by the two bus shafts during previous 48 waggons to return etc. destroyed(?) were so much difficulty — no M.O. hurt — but very incidentally — very few men (M.O.'s & orderlies) wounded by outside shrapnel fire — wounded during night 7187.	
ECOURES 12 noon 5 p.m.	Vichny very hot 7187. visit off a.d.s. & H.Q. — spent most of today. T.B.L. — so far as possible during the 5 hrs to new huts — arranged work & gunners during the 5 hrs. Sh. the huts to new huts surrounded(?) much to be done. tea before unloading men turned out etc. arrangements made to put up pence— loaded — Reserve bath — 7187.	
3. V.11 6.30 a.m.		
10.30 a.m.	LT MAROEUIL to discern hopeful find time upshot the bus— were very few grd.	
3.8 p.m.	visit off a.d.s. Particulars were got from hits — entries of G.S.E. letters 2 then of two twenty itself — need most stirring corps patients	
6.30 p.m.	left active throughout mn. T.B.L.	
	Cars lr. & lt a/F arrived a.d.s. 11 p.m. mostened of 9.25 p.m. no trouble at all. 7B.L.	

MEDICAL.

60

Vol 3

Aug. 1916.

CONFIDENTIAL.

WAR DIARY

Vol 3 Pages 10 to 14.

of

MAJOR T. B. LAYTON, Commanding

2/4th LONDON FIELD AMBULANCE.

COMMITTEE FOR THE
MEDICAL HISTORY OF THE WAR
Date -5 OCT 1915

War Diary. Vol. III. Appendix I.
2/4 London Field Ambce.

ORGANIZATION
OF
ADVANCED DRESSING STATION.

Map Reference
France 1/40000 N°. 51B.

A 8 c 5. 6.

The Dug-outs will be used as follows:-

No	In Ordinary Times.	In Emergency.
1	Overflow Ward for Stretcher Cases or Billet for Visitors or Excess Personnel.	Ward for serious stretcher cases.
2	Dressing Room for stretcher cases.	Dressing Room for stretcher cases.
3	Ward for stretcher cases	Ward for stretcher cases not serious.
4	(i) Ward for Sick Parade. (ii) Ward for cases waiting to walk down in event of shelling	Ward for walking cases.
5.	Med. Inspection Room & Dressing Room for lightly wounded	Dressing Room for Walking Cases.
6.	Billet for Personnel.	Ward for Stretcher cases not serious.
7.	Officers Mess.	Ward for Officers Walking cases.
8.	Officers Billet	Ward for Stretcher cases. Officers

SHELTERS:

No	In Ordinary Times.	In Emergency.
9	Lying cases waiting to be dressed.	Lying cases waiting to be dressed.
10.	Pack Store.	Pack Store.
11	Patients waiting to walk down.	Collecting Place for cases to be evacuated.

PARA 2.
ENTRANCES:-
- (A). Entrance (from Territorial trench) for all stretcher cases.
- (B). Exit for cases from DUG-OUT Nº 1. Entrance for personnel to DUG-OUTS Nºs 1 & 2.
- (C). Exit from DUG-OUTS Nºs 2 & 3.
- (D). Entrance for Personnel to DUG-OUTS Nºs 3, 4 & 5 & SHELTERS Nºs 10 & 11, — for Patients — walking cases, to DUG-OUTS Nºs 4 & 5 & SHELTER Nº 10 & for all wounded to SHELTER Nº 11.
- (E). Entrance & Exit for Personnel to DUG-OUTS Nºs 4, 5 & 6 & to COOK HOUSE. Exit from SHELTER Nº 11.
- (F). Entrance & Exit for Patients to DUG-OUT Nº 6, & Patients & Personnel to DUG-OUTS Nºs 7 & 8.

NOTE:- This arrangement is based on the following principles:-
(i) To keep Entrances separate from Exits as far as possible.
(ii) To keep sick & slightly wounded who do not need instant attention, from seriously wounded who do need it.
(iii) To prevent administrative arrangements of Cooking & Pack Store work, from being interfered with by a crowd of Patients.
(iv) To prevent Patients & Personnel continually hanging about on the road outside the A.D.S.

cont.

bench E by the Orderlies looking after the sitting cases.
Intermediate cases should be put in DUG-OUT N°3.
Wounded Officers will be dressed in DUG-OUTS N°s 2 or 5 as the case may be & must then be brought out of the Dressing Stn. along the road & TRENCH F & then to DUG-OUTS N°s 7 & 8.

<u>In ordinary times.</u>
SHELTER N° 11 may be used for sitting cases waiting to be evacuated, provided the Dressing Stn is not being shelled.

<u>During an engagement</u>
This Shelter would probably be useful to collect Patients lying or sitting who are the next to be evacuated.

<u>AT ALL TIMES</u> It is of the utmost importance that neither Patients nor Personnel should be allowed to hang about at the Entrances to the Trenches & on the roadway, in the way they do at present.
In ordinary times they can readily be seen from the enemy's kite balloons & are a source of danger to the Dressing Stn & the whole area surrounding it.
During an engagement the road outside the Dressing Stn, will probably be subjected to continuous shell fire & will be very liable to a serious block, from motor ambulance wagons turning round & from vehicles passing backwards on the light railway.
It is only by constant care during ordinary times that serious congestion will be avoided at this spot during an engagement

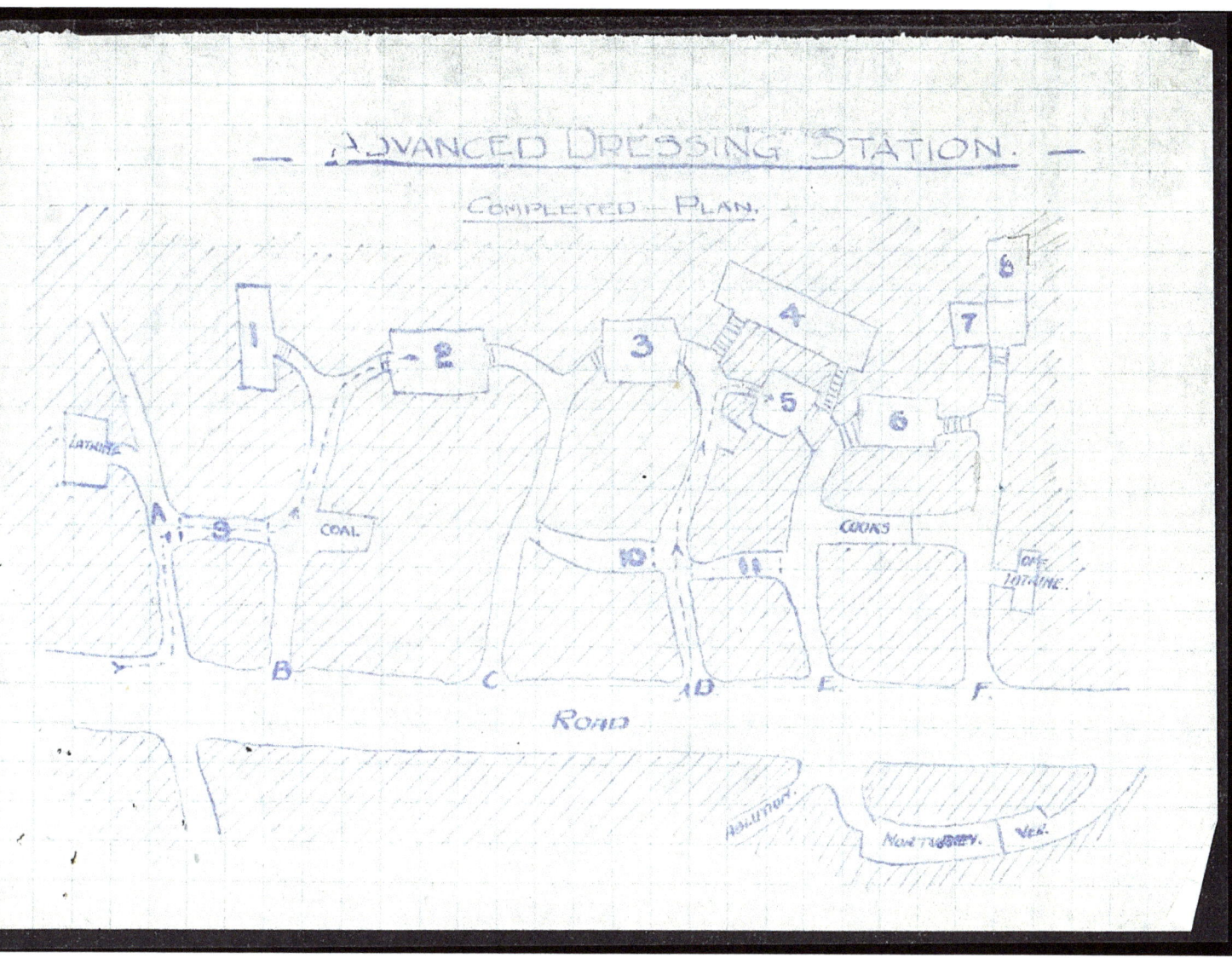

PARA 3.

In ordinary times

DUG-OUT Nº 4, is to be kept quite empty, except for Patients
At Sick Parade they will go down into this DUG-OUT by the steps from trench D. & will then come up, one by one, by the other steps until seen by the M.O. in DUG-OUT 5.

If it is decided to evacuate them, they will then go to SHELTER 11, & wait there until it is time for them to walk or ride down, unless the A.D.S is shelled, in which case, they will be told to return to DUG-OUT Nº 4.

Patients walking down in batches from the Collecting Posts & R.A.P's. will follow the same route until seen by the M.O.

During an engagement.

Walking cases will enter by the same trench, be dressed in DUG-OUT Nº 5 & go down to DUG-OUT Nº 4 from TRENCH D.

Food should be issued while in the DUG-OUT, the Orderlies going down by the steps from TRENCH E.

Men who have been fed & are the next to be evacuated will be collected at this end of the DUG-OUT coming out by the steps to TRENCH E & thence either to SHELTER 11 or directly onto the road.

In ordinary times.

Stretcher cases will be admitted through TRENCH A, to DUG-OUT Nº 2, where they will be dressed & carried on to Nº 3, overflowing into Nº 1 if need be.

During an engagement.

Stretcher cases will be dressed in the same DUG-OUT & the most serious cases taken into Nº 1, the least serious cases must be brought out of the DRESSING STN along the road & through TRENCH F to DUG-OUT Nº 6, where they can be fed from

2/1 LOND. A.M.B.

WAR DIARY or INTELLIGENCE SUMMARY.
(Erase heading not required.)

Army Form C. 2118.
Vol III / S 10.
MEDICAL.

Hour, Date, Place	Summary of Events and Information	Remarks and references to Appendices
ECOIVRES 1.VIII.16. TUES 10.30 a.m.	Just arranging to visit the frontline morning — Busy arranging staff & new huts — 7M.L	RDMS called in my absence 7M.L
2.VIII.16 WED	Lt Capt BIRD returned, Capts Pryce, HARRIS & MILTON of ADS. Went with MM — about night. Saw L/Bayne to M+J R.A.P. counter in to Capt LINDELL Withdraw old post in Merckem. Thence own to S.E. corner of NEUVILLE ST VAAST — to collecting post — extend wire back to ADS — 20th Inf Brigade used return thence morning whole round 4 to VTG to inspected quarters 7MDSM	
2.30 Conference C ADSM		
3.VIII.16 10.17p.	Saturday — routine work — 7M.L Friday — went on lower Limiten ACG — 2nd wall circular I.D. Took Squires car to AC 8 — wires recently Mr. Saw Kay — my party — as ams came around the 9ML — morning — SNYDER called — Qast Chap Gen called 9ML morning — Capt MINNETT taken activities on Div Baths 7ML	
5.VIII.16	Routine work. Very hot day. Capt. Pelley returned from Gas Course at St. Pol and went to Advanced Dressing Station. 7ML	
6.VIII.16	Hot day. Church Parade Capt. Kimber reported as Medical officer in charge to the 172 Tunnelling Coy. R.E's. 7ML	
7.VIII.16	Moved patients into new Huts. 7ML	
8.VIII.16	Work continued on new area for Dressing Station. 7ML	

2/4th Lond. Amb. WAR DIARY Vol III Page 11.   Army Form C. 2118.
or
INTELLIGENCE SUMMARY.
(Erase heading not required.)

Hour, Date, Place	Summary of Events and Information	Remarks and references to Appendices
9 VIII 16	Hot day His Majesty The King passed along road North of Main Dressing Station - all Patients sitting on Bank above Road, Ready and fallen in expecting that he would inspect our Dressing Station on the way back but he did not do so. 7PL	
10 VIII 16	Sergt. Major Perry and Sixteen men went up to Neuville St. Vaast to begin repairing old Trench up to O Section. 7PL	
11 VIII 16	Captn. Spencer and party at No. 42 Casualty Clearing Station returned for duty. Captn. Pritchard relieved Capt. Bird at Advanced Dressing Station. 7PL	
12 VIII 16	Hot day - Routine work. 7PL	
13 VIII 16	Captn. Price Harris relieved Capt. Petley at Advanced Dressing Station. 7PL	
14 VIII 16	Hot day - Routine work 7PL	
15 VIII 16	Captn. Spencer relieved Capt. Pritchard at Advanced Dressing Stn. 7PL	
16 VIII 16	Captn. Pritchard takes on Administrative Duties entirely - is in charge of cooking arrangements and Sanitary arrangements. 7PL	
17 VIII 16	Went up the line with Captn. Dupaine O.C. 17 Corps Light Railway He indicated where Light lines could be obtained in Neuville St. Vaast for laying same - Visited G.O.C. 180th Brigade to discuss Code for getting Motor Ambulances up to A.D.S. in cases of abdominal wounds Returned by Motor Trolley. 7PL	

2/4th Lond. Amb.

WAR DIARY
or
INTELLIGENCE SUMMARY.
(Erase heading not required.)

Army Form C. 2118.

Vol III Page 12.

Hour, Date, Place	Summary of Events and Information	Remarks and references to Appendices
18.7m.16	Fine day. JMH	
19.7m.16	Went round Front Line Trenches with Capt. Charles – Left A.D.S. 4 am, and visited N Sector just after "Stand to". D.A.Q.M.G. 17 Corps	
3 pm	A.A.& Q.M.G. Division with D.D.M.S. Corps and D.A.D.M.S. Division came round Main Dressing Station – Discussed accommodation – Orders to give up Hut at present occupied by Quarter Master – to make the most of accommodation in the billet and to build huts round remaining two sides of Admission Block for further accommodation. Told us that ultimately we should move out of present Harness Room but they would give us plenty of notice of this. JMH	
20.7m.16	Fine day. – Church Parade. Visited 28th Field Ambulance (Major Harty) JMH	
21.7m.16	Moved Medical Inspection Room into dark empty room near roadway by the Billet and put Dispensary store in the same place. Captn. Milton relieved Capt. Price Harris at A.D.S. JMH	
22.7m.16	Attended Conference of Officers at Office of A.D.M.S. JMH	
23.7m.16	Captn. Kimber returned from duty with Tunnelling Coy. Went up the line with Sergt. Major – New trench getting on well – Saw Lt.Col Sword O.C. 2/19th Battn and Lieut. Porteous and discussed question of putting down wide gauge and obtaining working party from 2/17th and 2/19th Battns. Visited A.D.S. still no attempt to alter it – Gave exact instructions to Captn. Milton as to rearrangement of same. JMH	
24.7m.16	Fine day. A.D.M.S. definitely decided to have narrow Gauge in	

2/4th Lond. Amb.

Army Form C. 2118.

WAR DIARY Vol III Page 13.
or
INTELLIGENCE SUMMARY.
(Erase heading not required.)

Instructions regarding War Diaries and Intelligence Summaries are contained in F.S. Regs., Part II and the Staff Manual respectively. Title pages will be prepared in manuscript.

Hour, Date, Place	Summary of Events and Information	Remarks and references to Appendices
24.VIII.16	evacuation Trench. Lt. Col Birkett O.C. 2/17th Battn not prepared to give fatigue party when in Divisional Reserve to help on our Trench.	JRL
25.VIII.16	Captn. Kimber relieved Captn. Spencer at A.D.S. G.O.C. inspected Main Dressing Station – very critical on Operating Theatre – Objected to Medical Inspection Room and to catering arrangements. In afternoon moved Medical Inspection Room and Quartermaster Store. Request from 2/14th Battn for eight extra Bearers. These sent – Visit to G.O.C. 179th Infantry Brigade to see if he needed any further Medical assistance – He deprecated Medical assistance being sent in such case and did not think I ought to have known of proposed raid.	JRL
26.VIII.16	Slight rain in morning – beautiful day with cool breeze. Went out for a ride with other Officers – Horse slipped when galloping, fell heavily on shoulder – apparently no serious injury. D.D.M.S. inspected M.D.S.	JRL
27.VIII.16	Fine day. Church Parade.	JRL
28.VIII.16	I went to No. 30 Casualty Clearing Station for Xray of Shoulder.	JRL
29.VIII.16	Work on operating Theatre – roofing of Huts continued, cookhouse being paved with bricks from old French Incinerator – Heavy Thunderstorm 4.30 p.m. 2 ft of water in Harness Room – Cookhouse isolated with water. Report of Xray – Fracture of Right Humerous. Captn. Howlett 2/5th Field Ambulance relieved Captn. Milton at A.D.S.	JRL
30.VIII.16	Continual rain. Saw Col. Gray, Consulting Surgeon 3rd Army	JRL

2/4th Lond. Amb.   Vol III Page 14.

Army Form C. 2118.

WAR DIARY
or
INTELLIGENCE SUMMARY.
(Erase heading not required.)

Hour, Date, Place	Summary of Events and Information	Remarks and references to Appendices
30 VII/16	He gave me permission to carry on subject to not exerting myself and not walking about in the Trenches. Drainage round Huts completed Pte. A.B.Carter – Fractured Radius (accidental) evacuated.	
31 VII/16	Fine day. Lt. & Q.M. C.L.Baynes evacuated to No. 42 Casualty clearing Station, diagnosis – Neurasthenia. Under instructions of G.O.C. new Hut let to us for Medical Inspection Room.	

MEDICAL

Army Form C. 2118.

WAR DIARY
or
INTELLIGENCE SUMMARY.
(Erase heading not required.)

Vol 4

CONFIDENTIAL

War Diary of 2/4 London Field Ambulance
Vol III pgs 15-19
September 1916

COMMITTEE FOR THE
MEDICAL HISTORY OF THE WAR
Date 26 OCT 1916

2/4 LOND AMB. WAR DIARY or INTELLIGENCE SUMMARY.   Vol III   Pg 15.   Army Form C. 2118.

Hour, Date, Place	Summary of Events and Information	Remarks and references to Appendices
Friday Sept 1st 1916. ÉCOIVRES.	CAPT MILTON 7p/c — LT C.L. BAYNES 7p/c Ole Coles (quashed by accidental) evacuated. Visited A.D.S. — found that arrangements made on outbreak of O/C being fully carried out. (Probably due to repeated change of O/C) Have just instructions sir CAPT KIMBER. Found new latrine for men completed — arranged new site for officers latrine. Old latrine to be converted into shelters. Machinery old officers latrine to be converted into shelters for nominal reduction. — sent S.M. PERRY who reports that made on Branch to hold up to ten men of armed times.	
Monday Sept 4th 1916.	CAPT PRICE HARRIS takes on duty on 6% of dispensary 7p/c. Visited Back shore and of half finished operation Room. Began to build sheds around yard of the [admission] Block. 7p/c.	
Wednesday Sept 6th 1916	Continued work at M.D.S. Began up notes on organization at A.D.S. 7p/c. CAPT PRITCHARD replaces CAPT HOWLETT at A.D.S. 7p/c. CAPT PRITCHARD discussed with CAPT PRITCHARD the work to be done. Visited A.D.S in accordance with Appendix I. Visited CAPT MINETT in filling up A.O.S the organization with him.	vide Appendix No I.
Thursday Sept 7th 1916	at MAROEUIL on my back a discussion of an engagement. Visited AUBIGNY & [illegible] of M.D.S in the event of an engagement. Visited AUBIGNY & [illegible] from O.C. 42nd C.C.S. authorization from for stretchers for use with THOMAS'S splint the supply of which has been required by ORDNANCE for use by FIELD AMBCES.	7p/c:-

MEDICAL.

2/4 LOND AMB.   WAR DIARY   VOL III PGE 16.
or
INTELLIGENCE SUMMARY.
(Erase heading not required.)

Army Form C. 2118.

Hour, Date, Place	Summary of Events and Information	Remarks and references to Appendices
Saturday 9th Sept. 16.	Visited AUBIGNY on return A.D.M.S & D.D.M.S. visited M.D.S. JPL	
Sunday 10th Sept. 16.	CAPT BIRD replaced CAPT KIMBER at A.D.S. D.D.M.S. visited large brown rat in officers mess & advised us to get an cat until large building of shed for transport. JPL	
Monday 11th Sept 16.	A.A. & Q.M.G. visited M.D.S. ordered me to change the site of Latrines incinerators & ablution bench belonging to the billet JPL	
Tuesday 12th Sept 16.	Boards in the Admission block have now both been repainted. P.O.M.S visited M.D.S. Discussed evacuation from A.D.S. & new widening the Rd. JPL	
5.15 am Wednesday 13 Sept/16	Took car up to be thoroughly examined trenches on night of L.I. Sector until & were to findining out where the patients could be more easily be evacuated from this part. Went up to SAPS overlooking LITCHFIELD CRATER. Visited HQRS 19TH BATTN do business with them the supply at Normal Solution. Examined work done by S.M. PERRY do man dressel for evacuation. Visited HQRS 2/15th BATTN (Not A.D.M.S. returned with hem do trenches & had already seen this morning) N visited HQRS 186TH BDE Returned M.D.S. 4 pm. Visited AUBIGNY in the afternoon. JPL	
2 pm Thursday 14th Sept 16.	Walked up SAPPER TRENCH to MAISON BLANCHE. Visited HQRS 2/15TH BATTN thence to HQRS 2/14TH BATTN in C.1. Sector. Visited M.O. 2/17 TH BATT in C.2. Sector thence to collecting post in NEUVILLE ST VAAST & A.D.S at 8. pm. Saw convoy arrive during wet rainy nght done by divisne JPL	

Army Form C. 2118.

2/4 LOND AMB. WAR DIARY VOL III PGE 17.
or
INTELLIGENCE SUMMARY.
(Erase heading not required.)

Instructions regarding War Diaries and Intelligence Summaries are contained in F.S. Regs., Part II and the Staff Manual respectively. Title pages will be prepared in manuscript.

Hour, Date, Place	Summary of Events and Information	Remarks and references to Appendices
Friday Sept 15th 16. Saturday Sept 16th 16.	By car to BRUMEHAUT FARM. 5.45 am. Examined ground above A.D.S. Drove to collecting party + back to A.D.S. for breakfast. — Thence to collecting party sector and up Physical trench. Congrats were fraternity of diggers & a new way from the back of the dugout where there is cover. — Possibly will shortly be cover along the station. — Numerous casualties though no bad for either side. Intake 754. Sent Stretcher-bearer report that a 2 to 3 hr intake during an attack was RIETZ Falling up also Shaffer & Loading to the road being worked for 2 hours. Unfortunately the ambulances had been sent to evacuate this evening & got away much the first load of patients before this Work resumed. 7 P.M. suffer the working parties the wanted during the afternoon off-work.	Capt PRITCHARD detached to duty with 2/21 st Batt
Sunday Sept 14th-16 Monday Sept 18th-16 Tuesday Sept 19th-16	Found with — greatly impacted constructed work. Lt. Col SRE Capt KIMBER returned for duty with 1/5 LOND AMB. Capt. J. SPENCER Co. ds. with 2/16 Batt. — Capt PRITCHARD returned 7 ML 5.0 am → by car to A.D.S. Then to NEUVILLE ST VAAST & front where Renault VIII crosses THELUS road (weather) back along the road till stopped by M.O. BRECON LINE only 1 st field way from there to road fork in the centre of the village. Thence to Co' suffer Tr. Saw EDINBURGH and BUY crators. Returned to A.D.S. evacy parts fallen in from 48 trs. hry drop rain. — I went with preparing partly 7 ML to in afternoon to new trolley line. Began new scheme shed at MDS. 7 ML.	→ J/400000 5/13 A.9.f.39. → A.9.a.4.9.

Army Form C. 2118.

2/4 Lond. Fd Ambs   Vol III VS. 18

WAR DIARY
or
INTELLIGENCE SUMMARY.
(Erase heading not required.)

Instructions regarding War Diaries and Intelligence Summaries are contained in F.S. Regs., Part II and the Staff Manual respectively. Title pages will be prepared in manuscript.

Hour, Date, Place	Summary of Events and Information	Remarks and references to Appendices
WED. Sept 20th 1916	Weather fine — men were drawing Shelter weather — Began a work next day in rest. JPL.	
THURS. — 21st 1916	Continuing work in my morning — sent Corp. RADMORE to ADS. to get in Shelter reads — also put Corp. PARKER on to operation room and left 3 bare shelters wih on new shed. M.T. + M.T. each to make their own shets. JPL	
FRI. — 22nd 1916	Inspection by D.M.S. at Army HQrs. Frisians were (1) Re the work not cleaned really enough (2) no tooth for men kept (3) Captain instructor at tolerated work. Shall I Pleid off advise). JPL.	
SAT. — 23rd 1916	Replaced Corp. STEADMAN at A.D.S. in evening work at ADS. — Cpl RADMORE has finished one set of shelter rods in Dry—one [?] — Bridge put down trenches road opposite trench B — several put in trench D to facilitate the space + made room for Lewis stores JPL	
SUN. — 24th 1916	Busy in the councils. From rain. by 9/16 Batt to ↑ at 8.9am to the busy. Port ↑ NEUVILLE. Hence to RAP. 12+L' Sectors + B.F. Reserve — off Sectors — saw trolley line much worse over the bedground. Thence to extreme sector. — Saw Capt SPENCER after the raid — hence etc. RAP. Saw cut-hand Train wounds in support line of sector to Thence to ARGYLLE Crater JPL.	
MON. — 25th 1916	Work at ADS. during S.R. for evening doing JPL. Came round Gas what needed — courage — or 2/4 2nd WCs	
TUES. — 26th 1916	Cpl PETLEY and 3 Sanit Corpal's came and went thoroughly round gas defence of ADS + both collection posts JPL.	Since last week weather has been fine. A bit of dew is promised from evening JPL
WED. — 27.9.16 3.30am	(written) Reconnaissance of the LUS road — knew it up Batrines to this Front ↑ to ZIVY Corner - could not get wheeled stretchers on / transfer a little with shutting down — thence round ADS. promises to play at HDMs + NEUVILLE - C.R.E. round ADS. promises to lay in watch here JPL.	

11am
(73989) W4141—463. 400,000. 9/14. H.&J.Ltd. "Forms"/C. 2118/10.

WAR DIARY
or
INTELLIGENCE SUMMARY.

(Erase heading not required.)

Army Form C. 2118.

1st Lond Arm[y] 1/5/19.

Hour, Date, Place	Summary of Events and Information	Remarks and references to Appendices
THURS - 28.9.16	On receipt of instructions from OC 1st Army RE stopped work on trolley line - put working parts to strengthen work - OC & OC RE went & arranged site for water tank - detectors in which stores was put on 23" wall - work letter to S.E of canal dump. Began on new work here to detectors - trod constructor 4 wire wheeled stretcher carriers sent up - now 10 in all 7PM.	
FRI - 29.9.16	Visited Town Major NEUVILLE ST VAAST to discuss situation of detectors not used site for new hutches - thence to detectors post cubic sector & RAP L sector - 11.9. C sector - saw new work hunt in several huts - thence to B's Res L sector - RAP L sector down trolley line - experiments front up to trolley bridge it 7PM.	
SAT 30.9.16		
noon	6 am - Ham - cards from scout of 1/15 Batt. with ADMS - Both collecting posts	
3 pm	OC 175 Lond Camb to IVY CAVE - hence to B's reserve HQ -	
8 pm	L sector were returned by Capt PETLEY and returned to M.O.S. 7PM.	
	NOTE: The diary of Sept 1st-16th is in the handwriting of Pte F. LUCAS co's orderly because troops dispatched to treating S/Sgt R. Heavens which we further with any [illegible] /B/Kenyon Major	

Oct 1916
went to Salonika
No's

60th Div

2/4th London Field Ambulance

140/17/88

Oct 1916

COMMITTEE FOR THE
MEDICAL HISTORY OF THE WAR
Date −2 DEC. 1915

MEDICAL.

Army Form C. 2118.

1/4 London Fd Ambul

pg 25   Vol 5

WAR DIARY
or
INTELLIGENCE SUMMARY.
(Erase heading not required.)

Instructions regarding War Diaries and Intelligence Summaries are contained in F.S. Regs., Part II and the Staff Manual respectively. Title pages will be prepared in manuscript.

Hour, Date, Place	Summary of Events and Information	Remarks and references to Appendices
	CONFIDENTIAL War Diary of 2/1st London Fd Ambulance from Oct 1st 1916 to Oct 31st 1916 (Vol III)	W Taylor Lieut 9/14 2/1 Lon Fd Amb

MEDICAL
Army Form C. 2118.

WAR DIARY
or
INTELLIGENCE SUMMARY.
(Erase heading not required.)

SHEET 1

Hour, Date, Place	Summary of Events and Information	Remarks and references to Appendices
ECOIVRES 1.X.16	Fine day - Spent morning forking up clybreak work wheel had arrived since lunch went away in afternoon to AUBIGNY No 30 & 42 C.C.S. There cars which bus twenty of the A.D.S. - Evening met to discuss in A.D.S. Colonel Park girl vide app 2.	
2.X.16	Spent morning with Capt PRICE HARRIS - Since gone from here away the north of the D.S. hospital arrangements precisely this affects kingage shifts in our camp Capt PRICE HARRIS also shewed full when he in charge Clair have it not with the evening conference DDT. Heavy rain not.	
3.X.16	Heavy rain - drizzled - rainy ok day and a the two points with the Twisty morning going on to trenches Teatin TRL putterly TRL	
7.0 am	walked with Rev Capt Macpherson D.A.D.S. - Say 1/4 inquisino regard	
9.0 am	were to assist as un know new day - out end cagain in week TRL with Capt PRITCHARD captured road through NEWVILLE & thence along THE LUB road to VISTULA tunnel (X 9.6.2.9) thence followed road by trenches to support two MILL STREET (X 10.a.57) examined TRT car again thence to RAP C° sulfate. Capt PRITCHARDS turned DD.R.S. to R.A.P. C° sulfate is south Capt KEARNS & STUBBS. thence it Roof auto sections - 180th T.B.D.* R.A. - 1/3 by R.E. & lifestyle huts in street. Collecting had HELOIYRES at 7.0 p.m. TRL Fine in afternoon TRL	
1/2 by	Experience transmit to work at H.Q.S. 179 v3 v° A/9.	
4.X.16	Routine work in inspey - to AUBIGNY in afternoon with liaison PINKERTON 1/18 best't & evenington with Dutch Surgeon Lt Smith Raing guy Fine in evening	
5.X.16	Heavy rain storm in with F - mature Cook - not deland RANDALL travel with an Chenex - Fine good days work MDL	

2/4th London Field Ambulance.

M.X 232
2nd October 1916.

MEMO ON ADVANCED DRESSING STATION AND COLLECTING POSTS.

1. The Staff at the A.D.S. consists of :-

    Two N.C.O.s, one a Sergeant. (N.B. The second of these is
        at present supplied by the 2/5th Lond. Amb.)
    One Corporal Back Store Keeper.
    Two Dressing Room Assistants.
    One Cook.
    One Cook's Assistant.
    Four Nursing Orderlies, one of whom looks after the Officers.
    Eight General Duty Orderlies, one of whom when on day duty
        assists in attending to the Officers.

    At each central Aid Post it consists of :-

    One N.C.O.
    One Cook.
    Eight bearers.
        N.B. When a working party is also living at a
        central Aid Post, a second cook is added.

II. The Dressing Room Assistant.

    One is allotted to each Dressing Room. They change
duty weekly.
    The Assistant i/c of No. 2 dug-out is on duty from 8 p.m.
till 12 noon. He is also responsible for the supply of dressings
and drugs to the A.D.S. and for forwarding of these to the R.A.P.s.
    He is responsible for the clerical work concerning such
cases as are dressed in his own dug-out, including sending
returns about these cases.
    When off duty he hands over the dug-out and cases
remaining which were dressed there to one of the nursing orderlies.

    The Assistant i/c No. 5 dug-out is on duty from 6 a.m.
to 10 p.m. He is responsible for obtaining the drugs and dressings
needed in his dug-out from the assistant in No. 2 dug-out.
He is responsible for the clerical work concerning such cases
as are attended to in his dug-out.
    He is also responsible for the general clerical work
of the A.D.S. other than that already mentioned.
    He is responsible for knowing how to work the telephone
and for seeing that someone is by this who also knows it when
for any reason he leaves his dug-out.
    When off duty he hands over the dug-out and cases
remaining which were attended to in it to one of the nursing
orderlies and is responsible for seeing that the orderly to whom
he hands over understands the telephone.

III. Clerical Work.
    The following clerical work only will be done at
the A.D.S.
    (a) Correct filling in of the Field Medical Card.
    (b) A record of A.T.T. of such cases only as are returned
        to their units.
    (c) A nominal roll of cases sent to any unit other

To be read and War Diary Vol III app 2.

            than our own M.D.S.
- (d) In the case of patients evacuated direct to a C.C.S. or Stationary Hospital a nominal roll in addition to that mentioned in "c" to accompany the patient.
- (e) Answering of memos.
- (f) Record of telephone messages sent and received will be properly entered on the white or pink form respectively.

IV. <u>Change of Duties</u>.

    The eight men sent each four days will move on as far as is possible in the following order :-

- (a) G.D.O.s at A.D.S.
- (b) Bearers at Collecting Post, Centre Sector.
- (c)   "   " C 1 and C 2 sub-sectors.
- (d) Working party.
- (e) Bearers at L 1 and L 2 sub-sectors.
- (f)   "   " Collecting Post Left Sector.

                                                    Major.
                                O.C., 2/4th London Field Ambulance.

WAR DIARY
or
INTELLIGENCE SUMMARY.

Army Form C. 2118.

SHEET III

Hour, Date, Place	Summary of Events and Information	Remarks and references to Appendices
ECOIVRES 14.X.16	Fine day - ordered to report to Junes at 9.30am - Discussed day's report of yesterday - am Inspected ar Units with Capt. I. - in afternoon to subject parts visited. Covers in 7/5, 3 & 2/12 Co.S. 7/B.L.	
15.X.16	Sunday - fine fine cold - Church parade - with Lt Col Kelly 6 Dublins - Inspected 7/16 Mont hosp. and T.C.S. - also B.R.C. store - to Donos some is slow of ? from there. (7/9L)	Capt Relly absent
16.X.16	Worked day - wrote operations report from London [word] - inspecting them - [words] with Capt RAZMONT & Lieut/Col PARKER on 6 other insp and Capt But at PDS. O.R. Section's Hd Qr. 7B.L.	
17.X.16	MEWVILLE 7/MSI - Inspect and overcased branch - FAUBIGNY - [words] 58th CITRESS & ice cell mine - at MDS. work continues - 7AUBIGNY 53th CITRESS & ice cell mine - lieut what orders work - have starts on all ? Jones. - LC Capt PEEBLES -	
18.X.16	2 PC mills at H our CCS became Trench work - indicators & died Raught under 7/9L. Inspected clearing - small cnwel spram 4 necessary - Inspected [word] & all mass at MDS - parks exhaust in short front in cold elections.	
19.X.16	Went with Capt. MILTON to ADS. Raining all day & upsets wth Capt MILTON to ADS Raining in ofts rain all day expects clothing at MDS, & both of Shelters to be clear with putty - Inspects all mines - wagons on way from arris of mine 2 went HQ MDS.	
20.X.16	Fine day but cold - at work with arms with HOM & covalter Got. On 10 but & Transig ham vistd m, DS. & Faschi Dur my field MDS - in afternoon - cnstirces - wandered on ch) Faschi and Farcuille in afternoon. 7/B.L.	
21.X.16	Major BAZIN & Tumson Sus Ambulance reported to Capfar to Inspect over tour hed - fine day - cold - with him interviewed MARQUEUIL to AUBIGNY ? 7/9L Fine day - cold met from Contuway in BAZON cuirous time dam 4+5 pm Carried Army	
22.X.16	Fine - Cold - packing all day. 9 Cunadian Aries cuartly wounder	
23.X.16	Lcn 12. 30 pm - Running and preparing station 8 pm 7/9L	

WAR DIARY
or
INTELLIGENCE SUMMARY.

Army Form C. 2118.

SHEET IV

Hour, Date, Place	Summary of Events and Information	Remarks and references to Appendices
ECOIVRES 24.x.16 7.40am	runners off TMK. hutted overnight forwagon to transport TMK	
ACQ. Bivouac 10.20am	received orders showing crews to billeting areas TMK	
BERLES-AU-BOIS	King halts TMK	
MONTI-EN-TERNOIS	Arrives TMK	
3.0pm 5.40pm 6.30pm	progressing TMK for inspection TMK	
25.x.16	wet & rainy day - cleared up towards evening - set up reception station - cleaned up farm where billeted - orders awaited TMK. finish rainy day census in D.of C. TMK	
26.x.16	Costa fine - some rain midday - bivouacs all were - replaced all transmitters - wagon sparred - reported to D.of C.	
27.x.16	179.13.57 in afternoon TMK much rain during night - sword rival speaking up - Capt PETLEY sent in to POTEL to arrange next day's blacks and escorted under R.Q.A. and orders - runaways for 179.B.Q. etc during night of sept. of General - 770Z	vide appx. 3.
28.x.16 FROTEL much	2nd day - some new tests - very St. S. Ossian TMK Arrived - Capt KINGSB R left 6 tanks with men posts - Capt MUVETT reported last night - Swamp station in swell hovel - all men billeted in farm meanwhile - two whiskies ailing away from its report to own 68th Div. - brought in sick with 3 hours whirls to return 1st6 steering hop my wheelie - sent patrols to aunts wagons wok 3 battalion GS wagons - heavy dust in Cant further than nothern TMK.	

WAR DIARY
or
INTELLIGENCE SUMMARY
(Erase heading not required.)

Army Form C. 2118.

SHEET V

Hour, Date, Place	Summary of Events and Information	Remarks and references to Appendices
FORTEL 28.X.16 cont. 4.0 p.m.	Capt PRITCHARD reported to B²⁰ HQ & received its instns as to billets &c from 7D¹.	
6.30 p.m.	Capt HUMBER rejoined from front. 2nd Lt TERVOS reporting that all ranges of M.G. are noted — also the instr. on to cuirasseurs holstergs and ℓ HL⁰ 3d encampment. Report to H²q. per S²e² Div. — and that the billeting area was to between GLISY & toby 7D¹.	
29.X.16	8.0 a.m. — horse ambulance wagon's fur-ball the horse & wrenched Loff. armed of studio cartridge (rds of P¹3) on fg P¹/L &c'sting shortly after moving off — moved heartily after this. 1h² moved — brigade stuck in squally route.	
	S.O. of ST ACHEUL M H² use too in 3 4²⁵⁻ Capt PETLEY arrived resting as S²e'park. 7D¹.	
1.45 p.m.	arrived PROUVILLE — rain stopped — formed transport station in CHATEAU — rest for rest &c 3p.m. 7D¹.	
6.0 p.m.	Capt PETLEY reported back & reports that all cases had been sent to 30³⁴ fd Amb. PREVENT — billy luny made return of men to Div Staff unty kong returned — all details cond-tin. 7D¹.	
PROUVILLE 10.30 p.m.	— worked parties in the morning wagon washing — cleaning band & bivouac Shelter — was funn'ng but interior all fretted with anti first-bite people — fragnunt showers — fine evening. 7D¹.	
30.X.16	H²/c. 179 and B²⁰ came to draw timber 7D¹.	
B²⁰ Fa 26 31.X.16	— working parties in morning — all wagons guns & &c cleaned — wherebel & wheel cleaned — cases inspected — DOOLIS²N Lry-hire and wagon. 7D¹.	
	Showery all morning — fine in afternoon — took all groundcloths were out for one hour. New type of Ant. 7D¹.	

/4 London Field Ambce
App III
War diary for Oct 1916
M X 296

MEDICAL ARRANGEMENTS for 179th Brigade and attached troops for the period 8 a.m. 28th October 1916 till morning of October 29th.

Two horse-wagons will march behind the 2/14th Battalion under Capt. SPENCER in accordance with Divisional Standing Orders para. 7, sub-para 20 (page 16).

This party will leave the column at VACQERIE le BOUCQ.

When the cases in these wagons have been dropped at the Dressing Station in FORTEL one of these vehicles will follow the 2/13th Battalion and one the 2/16th Battalion to collect any further cases that fall out and will remain with these Battalions under the Medical Officer until the morning of the 29th instant when they will return to FORTEL by 8 a.m. with any cases which need evacuation.

The third wagon will march at the head of the Field Ambulance and will follow the column when the Field Ambulance leaves this. One Corporal and one Private in addition to the wagon orderly will accompany this wagon and will be under the orders of the M.O. in charge Divisional Engineers.

The M.O. i/c Divisional Engineers will collect any cases which need evacuation on the morning of the 29th October from the following units:-

179th Brigade Headquarters
179th Light T. M. Battery
179th Machine Gun Company
2/4th London Field Company R.E.
2/15th Battalion

and will leave them under the care of the Corporal and Private detailed, informing the O/C 2/4th London Field Ambulance of the number and position of these men in order that he may arrange for their evacuation.

This ambulance wagon will march off on the morning of the 29th with the 2/4th Field Company R.E. rejoining the 2/4th London Field Ambulance when this joins the column.

All men and horses detached from the 2/4th London Field Ambulance will carry rations up to breakfast of the 29th October.

for Capt.
~~Major~~
O/C 2/4th LONDON Field Ambce

27/10/16.

Copy 3 of 9

Copy No: 1 Retained
" No: 2 Headquarters 179th Brigade
" No: 3 M.O. i/c 2/13th Battalion
" No: 4 M.O. i/c 2/14th Battalion
" No: 5 M.O. i/c 2/15th Battalion
" No: 6 M.O. i/c 2/16th Battalion
" No: 7 M.O. i/c 2/4th London R.E.
" No: 8 A.D.M.S.
" No: 9 War Diary. ✓

140/949

MEDICAL

Army Form C. 2118.

WAR DIARY
or
INTELLIGENCE SUMMARY.
(Erase heading not required.)

Instructions regarding War Diaries and Intelligence Summaries are contained in F. S. Regs., Part II. and the Staff Manual respectively. Title pages will be prepared in manuscript.

Hour, Date, Place	Summary of Events and Information	Remarks and references to Appendices
	CONFIDENTIAL War Diary of 2/4 London Field Ambulance From Nov 1st 1916 to Nov 30th 1916 Volume III	60th (London) Division. J B Taylor Lieut 2/4 London Fd Ambce to O/C 2/4 London Fd Ambce

2/4 London Field Amb

WAR DIARY
or
INTELLIGENCE SUMMARY
(Erase heading not required.)

Army Form C. 2118.

pg 25

Hour, Date, Place	Summary of Events and Information	Remarks and references to Appendices
BROUVILLE 1.xi.16	Inspection of all personnel by RAMC. What thought them fit for General [?] duty. at CLOSURES. JML	
	Unit went out on drill - some patients sent for scale	
	route - excursion to BOULENS. JML	
2.xi.16	My rainy day - MS. Pad dresses. Gave 21 units clothing - [?]	
	boots - found every units pair of ready [?] - inspected	For actual amounts
	packs up in afternoon - one fire next of unit of all men. JML	vide app. 304
3.xi.16 9.0am	Fell in - bright sunny morning -	
9.30am	wind off	
ST. RIQUIER 12.30am	- pouring through - one light D. house with ute left at 4.6 Div	
	ins. D. yrs tractor	
ENCOURT SUR SOMME 3.45pm	Arrived - hospital accommodation Small - so to ABBEVILLE to	
	see about [?] - only infants in the dept - Atendo	
	ST.(6) ETAPLES JML	CAPT MINE TT
4.xi.16	ST.(6) ETAPLES JML	detached as
	Fine day - found a chateau in EPANGE which would do for sick	O/c Div. Serial
	Soft outh to IP Division - [?] - among [?] mud [?] M.	Bn ctn
	DELETOILE. Some of meanwhile - the few inpatients continued.	JML
	as with, - cleansed unit in [?] - some [?]	
	orders received to prepare for move to the EAST in some	
	or E point Xii that	
5.xi.16	continued work at New Hospital - went to AMIENS in afternoon	
	Found place for evacuation in Brev. ETAPLES - found two	
	1 Lancashire Stationary Hosp. - Capt. MILTON OPg. JML	
6.xi.16	Handed in 7 hr Cargo & [?] G.S. wagons. JML	
	received permission to use cars -	
	[?] SPENCER takes command in Zugalornd. JML

74L

WAR DIARY or INTELLIGENCE SUMMARY

Army Form C. 2118.

1/1st London Field Ambulance Vol III pg 26

Hour, Date, Place	Summary of Events and Information	Remarks and references to Appendices
EAUCOURT-SUR-SOMME 7.XI.16	CAPT. A.R. SPENCER, left day. Continued as Sgt. in Champ, takes command. A wing but day continued. Raw. Work at Hospital continued: Surface drainage of grounds improved & put in working order. Interior of Hospital cleaned. Two cases only evacuated to C.C.S. A few discharged to duty. Very few admissions. P.U.O. chiefly. RS	
	CAPT. MINNETT, O/C Divisional Baths, arranges Battns. Accommodation in one of the outbuildings in the grounds at EPAGNE, acting on instructions from ADMS.	
	An impromptu Concert got up by members of Ambulance given RAMC & other troops in neighbourhood. 20.	
8.XI.16	Work at Hospital continued, cleaning of interior chiefly. About 8 evacuated to C.C.S. & 8 men discharged to duty.	
9.XI.16	There has been less rain today, but still very wet. RS	
10.XI.16	Work at Hospital, & more admissions. More patients are being sent into hospital. Temperature steady 940. P.	
11.XI.16	An eventful day but at night M. husband contains some rain. A few d. trains columns. Nothing L-M. Op-Shed. Rats numerous. RS Still in rest. A good many men PWO return from Fld Ambces. RS	

WAR DIARY or INTELLIGENCE SUMMARY

Army Form C. 2118.

9/4 London Artillerie   Vol III   ps 27

Hour, Date, Place	Summary of Events and Information	Remarks and references to Appendices
ENVOURT-SUR-SOMME 12.11.16	Returned from leave & re-assumed command — during my absence Lieut TE Rowe had joined as QM and Lt Curle Reyn had joined to replace Capt B S R D who had transferred to 162 Bgd N Lancs. Capt/QMR TER temporarily reverted to PS Pslt — Capt FAIRBAIRN Gds would do days as T.O. Sgt R. eac abandoned. Mr L.	
12 noon	Replied officers (normally) 72L	
4.0 pm	Attended 71 MRG to re-schedule e transfer of stores, guns 71L.	
6.0 pm	Reported at 119 Bgd HQ to Brig Gen Stevens on his learning assumed command that he was out 71L	
13.11.16	Received notice that we were to rejoin — busy packing 71L.	
14.11.16 8.15 am	Bivouacs fell in sect.	
9.0 am	Received all order — 9.25 am 71L moving H qrs — ABBEVILLE 71L	
11.0 am	Fell in — 11.15 am Transport leaving in 2 troops — 12 men marched off 71L	
LONGPRÉ 50p1	Arr Ste — but down trail — 4's transferred to 6's last trouble	
	Carried 71L Gt there wagons — Lory sustaining wt 6-7 Gds R	
	8.20 bivouaced to park in — 9.30 team watered (see F.P.O. B.17) 71L	
MONTE REAR 12 noon 15.11.16	2 hours by LT — horses cold up 71L — Sick men wD Derby well — by the by — Ol' return issued a good topic 71L wznk. Lunch from the weather 71L.	

Army Form C. 2118.

WAR DIARY
or
INTELLIGENCE SUMMARY.
(Erase heading not required.)

1/4 London Fd Amb Vol III
19.28.

Instructions regarding War Diaries and Intelligence Summaries are contained in F.S. Regs., Part II and the Staff Manual respectively. Title pages will be prepared in manuscript.

Hour, Date, Place	Summary of Events and Information	Remarks and references to Appendices
MACON 16.XI.16. 2-3:30am VIENNE 10am	Stopped for 3/4 hr — Littea issued to all ranks — animals watered again. T/Sgt. PHILLIPS — reported as having fallen out after train crossed bridge ago when trying to pass water — was sent up to Munijka Bistrica — left message with Station Master. 3 remnts halt — horses watered — littea to all ranks. T/R.	
PIERRETTE 2.45pm		
MARSEILLES 12:30am	Arrival — rugs let up — supplied fruits to entrain wagons of TMC. Capt. FRATLEY — 59 C.R. — with animals to one camp. Capt FAIRBAIRNS TMC.	
17.XI.16. 4:30am 10:30am	Remain to Camp CARSERUNNE — littea & cakes issued — T/R.	
18.XI.16.	Seven officers 3 officers allowed into town. Sevr of MG's into the town Stafford — Raining — day — camp very muddy and IRC. unpleasant — Leave taken out for rest until 3pm to all ranks. T/R.	
19.XI.16 11:30 2:15	2/Lt day but showery. T/R. Entered training quarters on MAT. TRANSYLVANIA IRC. Artillery Guns and entrained on T/ wagon	
AT SEA 20.XI.16 to 29.XI.16	See appendix 1/29.5. for details of voyage. T/R. Escorted on Journey by 3 destroyers — separate traffic to and on all times reported by TMS.	
30.XI.16. 11am L.35pm	Animals and energy T/R. — reported to T/MS. Guide who passed us to T/A.D.M.S. office — house in reserve vide app. 5.	
SALONIKA 4.30pm	Waited office camp — guide took us about 1/2 miles and saw Rest and Hampfleck, would divert us further — they started to surface to Swinnekitz camp, but the descent from which the Metric lorries were mine — they wagons arrived to our home trans us. Journee to Sal — all of whom will the us truck Mitown. T/R.	Apps. Retown Guaguelir Bivousaid in the NEVILLE STVYVHST area attacked TMC.

J.M.Layton
Major
OC 1/4 Lnd FdAmbRAMC

179th BRIGADE AND ATTACHED TROOPS.

Medical arrangements on the march November 3rd 1916.

1. A motor ambulance will report at Headquarters of the following units at 8 a.m. for the purpose of collecting such cases from morning sick parade as need evacuation.

        2/14th Battalion
        2/15th Battalion
        2/16th Battalion

The Medical Officer in charge 2/13th Battalion and 2/4th Coy. R.E. will arrange to send sick round to the present dressing station by 8.15 a.m.

2. One horse ambulance wagon will follow Brigade Headquarters, 179th Trench Mortar Battery, 179th Machine Gun Coy., 2/16th Battn., and 2/15th Battalion picking up casualties from these units.

This wagon will report to the O.C. 2/15th Battalion at 9.30 a.m and all cases picked up by it will be in medical charge of the Medical Officer i/c 2/15th Battalion.

This wagon will report back to the Field Ambulance at the end of the day with such sick of these units as cannot return to their battalions.

3. Two horse ambulance wagons will accompany the Field Ambulance to collect the casualties of the 2/13th and 2/14th Battalions, the 2/4th Field Coy. R.E. and the 2/4th Field Ambulance.

These cases will be in medical charge of Capt. PETLEY who will march before these vehicles.

A Lance Corporal and one Private will march behind these wagons as orderlies.

4. The wagon mentioned in para. 2 will continue to follow the column after the 2/15th Battalion have left it and will proceed via the cross roads SOUTH of U in BAELLANCOURT at which point further cases from Brigade Headquarters, 179th Trench Mortar Battery, 179th Machine Gun Company and 2/16th Battalion may be dumped. It will be accompanied by a Lance Corporal and a Private R.A.M.C. to act as orderlies.

2/11/1916.

Major,
O/C 2/4th London Field Ambulance.

Copy No: 1 A.D.M.S.
Copy No: 2 Headquarters 179th Infantry Brigade
Copy No: 3 O/C 2/13th Battalion
Copy No: 4 O/C 2/14th Battalion
Copy No: 5 O/C 2/15th Battalion
Copy No: 6 O/C 2/16th Battalion
Copy No: 7 O/C 2/4th London Field Coy. R.E.
Copy No: 8 War Diary
Copy No: 9 Retained.

2/4 London Field Ambulance
War diary page III   Appendix 5

DAILY DIARY of M.O. i/c troops H.M.T. 'TRANSYLVANIA'.

SUNDAY 19.11.16 Met all M.O's of 60th Division on board at 6.15 p.m. and discussed how inoculations should be carried out.
 a. I arranged that Capt. SPENCER of the Field Ambulance should take on the work of inoculating the officers and should also assist Capt. LADELL in doing the same for the 2/16th Battalion.
 b. I arranged that Capt. PRITCHARD should similarly help Capt. NIELSON with the 2/13th Battalion.
 c. I appointed Capt. KIMBER to act as M.O. i/c all details having no M.O. of their own. These included:-
  i. 2/4th London Field Coy. R.E.
  ii. Detachment of 60th D.A.C.
  iii. H.Q. 179th Inf. Brigade with Signal Section
  iv. 2 Coys. 2/15th Battalion London Regt.
    (in all about 700 men)
and arranged that Capt. MILTON should assist him in the inspections and inoculation of these details.
 d. I arranged that Capt. PETLEY with Lieut. CURLE should carry out the inoculation of the 2/4th London Field Ambulance.
 The question of doing cholera, typhoid and small pox vaccinations all at one time was discussed. The concensus of opinion was that this should not be done and those who thought it might be tried did not feel that it could be carried through as the troops would probably not agree to it.
 It was therefore decided to begin by doing the first dose of cholera, then, after 48 hours, doing T.A.B. in such cases as it was necessary if there were time and doing small-pox inoculation at the same time as the last dose of any other injection. It was recognised that it would probably be impossible to do any small-pox vaccinations on board.
 Capt. MILTON was put in charge of the hospital.
 Medical Inspection Rooms were allotted as follows:-
 2/13th Battalion - Female Infectious Diseases Room
 2/16th Battalion - Male   do: do: do:
 Details under Capt. KIMBER - corner of Hospital
 2/4th London Field Ambulance - Dispensary.

8.30 p.m. Officers inoculated against cholera including the two battalion commanders, the C.R.E. and several other senior officers.

20.11.16. Some motion on the part of the ship - rain during the day - result a large number of the men ill. Very difficult to get a move on with anything.
 Inspection of all on board - no venereal disease found.
 Sanitary inspection - morning - mess rooms very dirty - tables being cleaned but floor left owing to responsibility not being fixed - obtained fatigue party to clean floors. Tendency to close ports unnecessarily. Instructed various N.C.Os to keep same open.
 Afternoon - Mess Room had been cleared up - about 25 officers inoculated - some O.R's of Field Ambulance.

21.11.16. Fine day following rough weather last night - general tendency to recover from sea-sickness. Inspection with ship's Captain and O.C. Troops (G.O.C. 179th Inf. Brigade) - whole ship insufficiently cleaned and beginning to be very dirty. O.C. Troops met all O.C's with result that responsibility for various areas was more clearly defined and apparatus for cleaning more evenly distributed. Especially useful are following two points:- (a) all other ranks to be on deck till inspection is over so as to give working parties room in which to work, (b) Mess Rooms definitely allotted by areas and not by hours - hence possibility to fix responsibility for uncleanliness.

Afternoon inspection - all ranks had worked hard and with a few minor exceptions ship was moderately clean.

Inoculations. Field Ambulance three-fourths finished. 2/13th and 2/16th - about 100 men each done.

Officers

22.11.16. Fine day - arrived Malta 10.45 a.m. and remained there all day.

Morning inspection - ship clean - dining room allotted to details of Brigade Headquarters very dirty - serjeant of 2/4th Field Ambulance put in charge of it.

Hawkers from shore selling cigarettes, chocolate and oranges. I did not stop it as these seemed harmless.

Afternoon inspection - much paper on decks as a result of the hawkers.

Inoculations. Field Ambulance finished except for a few odd men.- 2/13th and 2/16th Battalions half finished - details under Capt. KIMBER half finished - officers complete except G.O.C. 179th Infantry Brigade, who does not wish to be done, and 2 M.Os who are too busy at present.

6 officers inoculated with T.A.B.

Evening. Capt. MILTON reports that hospital is full with patients all of whom have raised temperatures to-night. This probably due to the heat and stuffiness of the ship with all port-holes closed and no movement, preventing ventilation.

23.11.16. Still at Malta - many officers and other ranks have slight sore throats not enough to attend sick parade, probably due to deficient ventilation from the ship not moving. Went round before breakfast and ordered port-holes to be opened.

Found at inspection that cold air could be sucked through the ship. Arranged for this to be turned on as soon as the port-holes are closed at night.

24.11.16. The men have now been since Tuesday November 14th without any exercise - viz: November 14th 3 p.m. to November 17th 4.30 a.m. in train or at railway stations; November 17th-19th in Camp Carcassone, Marseilles without being able to go out. November 19th to now on board ship. I have advised that men be taken ashore and sent for a route march if possible. O.C. Troops is in agreement but thinks difficulty of landing and re-embarking 3000 men may be considerable.

Ship sailed from St. Albions Bay to Grand Harbour, Valletta arriving there at noon. Officers and Warrant Officers allowed ashore. O.C. Troops is applying to authorities for permission to let men go ashore.

Sterilization of clothes of lousy men carried on all day, apparatus allotted to 2/16th Battalion for this purpose.

Baths definitely allotted to units at certain times so as to see that every man gets one.

25.11.16. Gale in the night. Bow of ship broke loose in the harbour. Not sailing to day.

Refusal on part of ~~local~~ military authorities to allow N.C.Os and men ashore. Reported to D.M.S. office.

In the evening small epidemic of diarrhoea associated with severe abdominal pains and vomiting in some cases.

Opened men's infectious ward for purpose of treating them, M.O. i/c 2/16th using female infectious ward as inspection room.

26.11.16. Meeting of all M.Os 9 a.m. to discuss diarrhoea epidemic. 11 cases admitted last night from all units except 2/16th Battn. 2/16th Battn. has 12 cases on sick parade this morning - none serious. Other units had 6 cases on sick parade.

In all these cases the symptoms came on at about 3 p.m. after having had tinned meat and tinned peas for dinner. All cases are getting better.

Arranged that Capts. SPENCER and LADELL inspect the Steward's store to day to see whether any is under suspicion, and that the Orderly Officer of the Field Ambulance attend in the galley daily at 12 noon to see food before issue.

Also arranged that as we seem to be likely to stay here some time that T.A.B. inoculations be carried on where necessary. O.C's 2/4th London Field Coy. R.E. and 2/15th Battn. (2 Coys.) will not have their men done while on board, but we can carry on with officers - 2/13th and 2/16th Battalions.

Arrangements were made to take all men ashore for a route march. Men fallen in and kept there for 2 hours when news was received that arrangements to take them ashore could not be made. This a great pity.

27.11.16. Left Valletta Harbour at 10 a.m.

All cases of diarrhoea have recovered, and ward for them is again closed down. Blankets used for these cases all sterilised.

At morning inspection accommodation area on 'F' Deck, which has no port-holes, was very stuffy. Arranged to get hatches off and to put down a 'windsail'.

Too many cases in hospital. In future I shall not admit cases suffering from pyrexia and nothing more but detain them on Poop boat deck where they will probably do better.

Inoculation with cholera vaccine (2nd dose) begun. Dispenser serjeant reports that there are only about 200 doses on board.

28.11.16. Day much taken up with boat drills, hence no inoculations done. I have decided to do no more T.A.B. on board as it would mean that the men would be unable to march.

Ventilation still needs improvement. One windsail has been fixed on to one section of 'F' Deck. I have asked for one to be fitted on to each section but the Chief Officer says it would be dangerous as it would shew that we are a troop-ship.

8.30 p.m. Went round. Found that ventilation works well in the centre of the ship but has little or no effect at the ends. Asked Chief Engineer to see to this. He says that it is because the ventilators on deck are not trimmed properly to the wind and that this is the business of the Chief Officer. Saw Chief Officer who said that all ventilators had been trimmed to the wind earlier in the day but that our men had altered them. He promised to have it done again.

7 cases ptomaine poisoning among 2/16th Battn. apparently due to meat yesterday which was not tinned. All meat - tinned - inspected to day. Two tins condemned.

29.11.16. Found that air was turned on in hospital and partially in other places, but even then not completely all over the ship. All other ranks medically examined. There are no cases of venereal or infectious disease on board.

30.11.16.　　The following arrangements have been made for leaving the ship clean.
　　　a. The normal cleaning up will be done by the usual fatigues.
　　　b. A special fatigue has been told off to give a final clean up of all decks. Capt. PRITCHARD R.A.M.C.(T) 2/4th London Field Ambulance is in charge of these.

　　　Appended are:-
　　　1. Numerical roll of inoculations performed on board.
　　　　All M.Os have worked hard at these inoculations and have loyally responded to my frequent demands for them to do this work, while other officers have been off duty.

　　　2. A.F. - A27 - for the days 21st November to 29th November.

　　　3. List of cases to be dealt with on arrival.

　　4. Report on Infectious ~~sid~~ Disease.

　　　　　　　　　　　　　　　　　J. B. Layton

　　　　　　　　　　　　　　　　Major R.A.M.C.(T),
　　　　　　　　　　　　　　Medical Officer i/c Troops,
　　　　　　　　　　　　　　H.M.T. 'TRANSYLVANIA'.

H.M.T. TRANSYLVANIA.

Inoculations performed on the roy of officers

Unit	N° on Board	Chol. ½cc	Chol. 1cc	TAB ½cc	TAB 1cc
60 Div Staff	5	5	4	1	—
HQ 179 Inf B⁻	5	4	4	—	—
2/13 Batt L.Ry	38	38	36	—	—
2/15 - L.Ry	20	20	15	—	—
2/16 - L.Ry	35	35	12	—	12
4 Lond Fd Co RE	5	5	—	—	5
2/4 Lond Fd Amb	11	11	6	3	—
60 Div DAC	1	1	1	—	—
60 Div Sig. Coy	1	1	—	—	—
Other formations	18	1	1	—	—
	139	138	79	4	17

At Sea.
30.11.16.

J.B. Caufhmar
Major Rawnsley
o/c London Fd Amb
M.O. i/c Troops.

H.M.T. "TRANSYLVANIA" U.K.

Unit	Now bound	Cholera 1st dose	T.A.B.
2/13 Batt Lond. Regt.	930	916	215
2/16 do.	883	880	30
2/4 Lond. Field amb.	341	325	—
2/15 Batt Lond Regt.	386		
2/4 Lond Field Co's R.E.	210		
H.Q. 179 Inf Bde.	27	652	15
Signallers etc	20		
60 Div! Staff	4		
60 D.A.C.	17		
others	6	—	—
	2824	2773	250

J B Layton Major RAMC(T)
o c A.T. 2/4 Lon Field Amb.

(3)

H.M.T. TRANSYLVANIA
cases to be dealt with on landing.

synovitis of knee - R -   1.
cellulitis of hand - R -   1.
sprained ankle - R. -   1.
Inspiration   -
neuritis of foot ———   1
Bronchitis   -   1
P.U.O.   -   15

[signature]
Major
[signature]

H.M.T. TRANSYLVANIA.

MARSEILLES to SALONICA.

19th Nov to 30th Nov 1916

Return of Inoculations done on board.

Officers   238.
O.R.   3023.

Both T.A.B. & cholera vaccines used were supplied by the Royal Army Medical College.
Details on other pages

Salonica
30.11.16

JB Clayton
Major RAMC
O.C. Vaccinations
on H.T.

NOTES ON
EVACUATION OF WOUNDED in the NEUVILLE ST. VAAST area
by the
2/4th LONDON FIELD AMBULANCE,
June to October 1916.

[handwritten annotation: 2/4 London F'd Amb'ce / War Diary Vol III / Appendix 6]

PARA. 1.
The Field Ambulance evacuated the casualties on the line held by the 179th and 180th Brigades. The 179th Brigade held the centre sector extending roughly from A.16.c.5.6. to A.4.c.7.9. (Map 51B). The 180th Brigade from the latter point to S.21.B.2.2. Each of these sectors was sub-divided into a sub-sector held by one Battalion. R.A.P.s were approximately as follows:-

1. Centre sector, right sub-sector (C.1.) at A.15.d.2.8. This R.A.P. was usually occupied by the M.O. of the Battalion in Brigade reserve as well as that holding the sub-sector. Capt Stubbs of the 2/14th and Capt. Leech of the 2/15th were usually there.
2. Centre sector, left sub-sector (C.2.) at A.9.b.7.5. which was occupied alternately by Capt. Laddell of the 2/16th and Capt Hanks of 2/13th Battalions.
3. Left sector, right sub-sector (L.1.) at S.27.d.5.4. occupied alternately by Lieut. Porteus of the 2/19th Battalion and Capt. Legge Currie of the 2/17th Battalion until he was evacuated when Capt Clarke became M.O.
4. Left sector, left sub-sector (L.2.) at S.27.a.7.5. occupied alternately by Capt Churchouse of 2/20th Battalion and Capt. Churchill of 2/18th Battalion.

PARA. II.
From these R.A.P.s Field Ambulance bearers brought the patients to two Collecting Posts. That for the Centre Sector was in the Territorial Trench approximately at A.9.c.1.7. From C.1 Aid Post to this Collecting Post the the trench was along a road from A.15.d.w.i. to A.9.c.5.8. thence down Territorial Trench. The road there forms a wide trench covered with duck boards without many zig-zags and the carry was not a difficult one although it was about 1,200 yards.

From C.2. R.A.P. the carry was along Territorial Trench about 800 yards. It was however a most difficult one in a narrow trench where for part of the distance the stretcher had to be carried on the shoulders instead of the hands and where it was wide enough to carry the stretcher in the ordinary way there were numerous traverses. From this Collecting Post to the A.D.S. the carry was by Territorial Trench and included going underneath the ARRAS - BETHUNE Road at A.8.c.7.6.

That for the right sector was in NEUVILLE ST. VAAST at A.8.b.6.8. situated in a cellar of a ruined house. A trolley line runs from the R.A.P. (L.2) sector to the Road Junction A.3.c.3.9. thence along the road to the Road Junction A.8.b.2.8. thence to AUX RIETZ - NEUVILLE ST. VAAST Road and thence down to the A.D.S. From the R.A.P. L.1. sector it was a carry of 800 yards to the road junction A.3.c.3.9. whence it was possible sometimes to bring them by trolley line direct to the A.D.S. When this was not available, it was a long carry - 1,500 yards as the crow flies which probably means 2,000 yards by the trench.

From L.2. sector patients could be brought down all the way by the trolley line, which passed outside the

R.A.P.

PARA. III.

The A.D.S. was situated in dug-outs on the S.E. side of the MAROEUIL - NEUVILLE ST. VAAST Road   yards S.W. of AUX RIETZ cross roads and consisted of five trenches opening on to the road with dug-outs and trenches as shewn on the accompanying maps. The road outside the A.D.S. was   yards wide of which   yards were taken up by a line which goes up past this place.

Evacuation from the A.P.s to the M.D.S. was by Motor Ambulance at night time. Authority was given to send a motor ambulance to the A.D.S. by day in the case of urgent cases only.

PARA. IV.

When the area was taken over from the 1/2nd Highland Field Ambulance the following personnel was kept up the Line.

At the R.A.P.s C.1.   6 bearers
             C.2.   2 "
             L.1.   6 "
             L.2.   8 "

At the Collecting Post for centre sector
    1 Serjeant
    1 Corporal
    8 bearers.

At the Collecting Post for left sector
    1 Serjeant
    1 Corporal
    1 Cook
    1 General Duty Orderly
    14 bearers to act as reliefs for
        bearers of left sector.

At the A.D.S.
    2 Officers.
    1 Serjeant
    2 Corporals (1 for Pack Store
                 (1 for General Duties)
    1 Clerk
    1 Dispenser
    1 Cook
    2 Nursing Orderlies
    2 General Duty Orderlies.
    10 bearers to act as reliefs to
        stretcher bearers of centre sector

In addition a motor cyclist was kept up there for bringing messages down to the M.D.S. or to three cars which were kept at F.26.b.9.9. (Map sheet 51 C) where the drivers, wagon orderlies and one other man of the R.A.M.C. lived in a shelter.

The M.D.S. at ECOIVRES was used by the 1/2nd Highland Field Ambulance only for the admission of local sick and all cases from the A.D.S. were evacuated direct to a Field Ambulance stationed at HAUTES AVESNES which is (E.28.)

PARA. V. Orders were received for this Field Ambulance to evacuate through its own M.D.S. the cases from the A.D.S. as well as the local sick.

To do this efficiently it was clear that the unnecessary large staff up the line could not be spared from the M.D.S. and this was effected in the following way:-

(a) Four bearers only were sent to each R.A.P. and

the reliefs for these at the A.D.S. and
Collecting Post left sector were reduced to 8
each.

(b) At the Collecting Post for the centre sector
seven bearers were sent instead of eight and a
Lance Corporal instead of a full Corporal
At a later stage this Post was several times worked
with a Corporal and eight bearers without a
Serjeant

(c) At the Collecting Post left sector a Corporal
and a General Duty Orderly were cut out as it
was felt that the bearers acting as reliefs
could very well do all the necessary work.

(d) At the A.D.S. the second Corporal was replaced
by a third Nursing Orderly. In this way 19
men were brought back from the Line.

(e) The Wagon Rendezvous at F.26.c.9.9. was
done away with and the motor cyclist was no
longer kept at the A.D.S. This Wagon Rendezvous
appeared totally unnecessary. Orders were
received from the D.D.M.S. that the MAROEUIL -
AUX RIETZ road was only to be used by day
to bring down cases of wounds of the abdomen
but this was extended to such cases of haemorrhage
which could not be controlled by manipulative
measures and which the M.O. thoughtshould be
operated on immediately. In this way the extra
man at the Wagon Rendezvous became available
for duty at the M.D.S. and the cars with their
wagon orderlies and drivers could be used for
evacuating urgent cases from the M.D.S. instead
of keeping continually on duty another car
at this place.

PARA. VI.

The route which the cars used to take to the A.D.S. was through
MAROEUIL and thence by the Fme Brunhaut to the A.D.S.
where they had to turn round in order to come back. This
last is a most difficult procedure as the car has to back
several times in order to get round and in doing so must
get the back wheels across the light railway leading to
the possibility of the whole road being blocked supposing
a car broke down while the turning was in process. An
attempt was made to obviate this by sending the cars up one
way and bringing them back by the AUX RIETZ - LA TARGETTE
cross roads and thence by the road to the cross roads at
~~~~~~~~~~ F.15.a.0.7.

This however had to be given up owing to the difficulty
at these last cross roads. At this point two trolley lines
converge on to the Engineer Dump and the road goes
steeply down hill through the wood and is quite dark except
for the light from hurricane lamps in the hands of people
moving about and which only tend to make it more difficult
rather than easier. Further the cross roads both at AUX
RIETZ and LA TARGETTE are both dangerous corners as is
also the road between them.

It was therefore finally decided to send the cars
up and down by the route ECOIVRES - Road junction at
F.14.a.9.7. - Road junction F.15.d.6.1. - Fme Brunhaut -
A.D.S. and the danger of turning was reduced to a minimum
by making all cars draw in as close as possible to the N.W.
side of the road and one turning at a time and doing no

- 4 -

loading until the whole convoy had turned.

PARA. VII.
The next thing that was done was to try and make more easy the evacuation from the R.A.P. of L.1. sector to the A.D.S.

In the area occupied by the FOSSE CHARBONNE (A.3.a.) were numerous disused French trenches opening on to the QUARRIES road between S.27.a8.2. and A.3.c.3.8. These were reconnoitred by me with the aid of Pte. F.LUCAS on July 26th and the attached report was sent to the A.D.M.S.

After reconnoitring these trenches himself with G.S.O.1 of the Division the A.D.M.S. decided to have the line laid down along the trenches Cii above.

Permission was obtained for this to be done and the O.C., XVII Corps Light Railway said that we might pull up the existing 40 c.m. railway line in the town and relay that.

This work was begun on Aug. 8th by Serjt. Major P.J. PERRY with a party that varied from 10 to 16 men according to the number that could be spared. This party lived at the Collecting Post NEUVILLE ST. VAAST and the greatest credit is due to all for the way in which they worked, and specially to Sergt.Major PERRY who directed the whole. When the line was ready to lay a report was sent to the C.R.E. advising that it should be laid on sleepers and the line ballasted, but he did not approve of this as he feared he could not provide the material. He said that we must do the best we could with the chalk which we could carry up from the QUARRIES.

The existing line in NEUVILLE ST. VAAST was not enough for the purpose especially in regard to small curves. However more line was discovered in a corner of the railway dump at the BOIS DE BRAY and was sent up.

In the meantime the Os.C. the Battalions that held L.1. sector had become interested in the line and some labour was got from them in making it, an agreement being made that when complete it should be used for taking up rations and ammunition to this sector.

At the end of seven weeks the work was nearly completed when a message was received from the O.C., 1/6th London Field Coy., R.E. that he had orders from the C.R.E. to take over the line next day in order to lay it on sleepers and put down ballast. therefore

My working party was withdrawn and nothing was done for another ten days when the engineers began work on it and at the time that the Division left the area the line was just completed.

Five small sidings in all were put in, one at either end to assist in loading, one about 100 yards from the front end into which the ration trolleys could be put for unloading and two intermediate ones to facilitate passing.

Some old French trolleys were collected, and were adapted by Capt TAYLOR, 1/6th London Field Coy. R.E. so as to take two stretchers the lower being put in as in 'load wagons' the upper being lifted on.

About 20 yards S. of the point where this trench - which we named DOWSETT DRIVE - came out on to the Quarries Road, was another disused trench. During a wet period when he could not employ the men on DOWSETT DRIVE Sergt. Major PERRY dug out the first 66 feet of this so as to make a space 10 ft. by 10 ft with a view to using it as a place for the keeping and attending to patients at any time

that might be necessary. This proved to be of the greatest
value as on Oct 11th the XVII Corps authorities were
looking for further medical accommodation in this part of
the line and seeing this place ordered me to get on with
the work there. It was designed to take 30 lying patients
or over 40 sitting as well as having a dressing room and
a cook-house (plan attached). It became known as PERRY'S
PALACE and when we handed over the water was laid on, all
the timber collected to construct it and some 600 sand-bags
ready to put on top when made.

DOWSETT DRIVE was just finished in time to use being
handing over.

PARA. VIII.

Evacuation from C.2. sector was never satisfactory, but so
far as the Field Ambulance was concerned no working party
could be got to improve it.

PARA. IX.

The question of evacuation in the event of an advance was
considered. From the map it would seem clear that the road
NEUVILLE ST. VAAST - LES TILLEULS - THELUS would be useful
for C.2. and L.1. sectors and it was reconnoitred from
this point of view.

From the A.D.S. to the point A.9.a.4.9. the road
was in such a condition that with little clearance motor
ambulances could be brought up to this point. From here
to the bend at A.9.a.5.6. the road was very bad with
shell holes which became more numerous as time went on
and scattered with debris from surrounding houses.

It was crossed by three trenches DENIS -LAROQUE - BRECON LINE
and a small one between these: the first was already bridged,
for the other two I had timber prepared so that it could be taken
up on wheeled stretchers and a bridge put across each with
very little labour.

This piece of the roadway could have been made passable
to wheeled stretchers by means of a large working party working
during one night.

I had intended taking up 100 men in ambulance cars
immediately after dusk and working at it all night.

From A.9.a.5.6. to the point where VISTULA and
PARALLEL 8 crossed the road it was passable for wheeled stretchers
Beyond this point it was absolutely protected from the sight of the
enemy for another 100 yards where it turned to the right and
ran direct towards the German lines and was visible from
there. Its surface however was still good enough for
wheeled stretchers and where it was crossed by RIETZ and
GUILLEMONT TRENCHES these were bridged.

It could therefore have been used right up to MILL STR.
by us without asking for any R.E. or other help.

I concluded that this road might be used under the following
circumstances:-
- a. During winter and hazy weather patients could have been
  brought from VISTULA TRENCH on a wheeled stretcher all the
  way to the A.D.S. when the road had been repaired in the way
  indicated.
- b. In an attack it would probably have been safe to use the
  road from RIETZ Trench then to have evacuated by AUX RIETZ
  or DENIS LAROQUE. I pointed out these points to MAJOR
  BAZIN of the 4th Canadian Field Ambulance when he took
  over from me and suggested that a new R.A.P. for C2 sector
  should be made in VISTULA Trench so as to make use of this
  road.

c,   If an attack had been pushed home this road passed
        very near the ZIVY cave which might have been used as
        an A.D.S.   I could have got some equipment up to this
        point in a limber wagon by man handling it.
           This last point I did not discuss with other
officers.

T.B. Layk
Major
OC 1/1 London Field Amb

30-11-16.